What's the Point, What's the Purpose

Seeing Faith Through the Simplicity of Love

Cindy H. Carr, D.Min, MACL

This book is published by CHC Connect.

Printed in the United States of America
First Edition, 2025

ISBN: 978-1-971192-00-0

For permissions or inquiries, contact:
Cindy H. Carr
cindyhcarr@outlook.com
www.cindyhcarr.com

Acknowledgements

Writing this book has been a journey of reflection, learning, and gratitude. I am deeply thankful to the many people whose wisdom, support, and encouragement made this work possible.

To my family — Dubby, DeEbra, and Jessica — your love and patience have sustained me through the long seasons of writing, research, and ministry. You have been my constant reminder of God's faithfulness and grace.

To my mentors, colleagues, and friends who have served alongside me in ministry, thank you for modeling authentic compassion and Christlike leadership. Your partnership in caring for the broken and weary continues to inspire me every day.

A heartfelt thank-you to Wendy J. Miller, my spiritual director and advisor throughout my Masters and Doctor of Ministry programs. Your wisdom and presence guided me with both gentleness and truth, helping me to see God's work even in the most challenging moments.

Table of Contents

Preface

Every book begins with a stirring — a quiet whisper from the Spirit that says, "It's time to speak." This book was born from that kind of whisper. I have spent my life in ministry — studying theology, preaching, pastoring, and walking beside people in every stage of faith. I've watched hearts come alive in the presence of God, and I've watched others quietly drift away, not because they stopped believing, but because they grew weary of the noise that sometimes surrounds belief.

For years, I wrestled with the same questions they did: What's the point? What's the purpose? The more I learned about God, the more I realized how much I didn't know — and yet, how much He loved me anyway. I found that the heart of the Gospel isn't found in mastering doctrine but in embodying love.

I wrote this book for those who are asking questions, who love God but struggle with the divisions that often come with faith. I wrote it for those who have stayed and those who have left — because both are still part of the same story. When I began studying theology, I thought knowledge would bring certainty. Instead, it brought humility.

It was in that humility that God spoke to my heart one day: "From now on, preach what you stand for—not what you stand against." That single instruction reshaped everything. It changed my ministry, my message, and my heart. I began to see that love was not simply a topic—love is the point and purpose behind every revelation of God. This book is my way of sharing that journey: moving from argument to listening, from division to connection, from fear to freedom. It is written for every person who struggles with the complexities of religious messaging.

In these pages, you'll explore questions of theology, history, and community—always through the lens of love. You'll find reflections on why theology divides and how love heals. You'll discover the courage to build faith communities that look like Acts 2—authentic, simple, and full of life.

And through it all, I pray you'll discover or rediscover a God who is more beautiful, more loving, and more present than you ever imagined. This isn't a book of answers; it's an invitation. An invitation to think deeply, to love freely, and to follow Jesus beyond the boundaries of certainty — into the mystery of grace.

If you've ever questioned your faith — welcome. If you've ever felt out of place in the Church —

welcome. If you've ever loved God but struggled with His people — welcome. This book isn't about rebuilding religion. It's about rediscovering relationship.

You are not alone in your doubts, and you are not disqualified by them. God isn't afraid of your questions — He's drawn to them. He meets us in the asking, and in that space between what we know and what we hope for, His love does its deepest work.

So as you turn these pages, don't rush. Pause where something stirs. Reflect when something challenges you. Let this be more than reading — let it be worship. Because the point and the purpose of it all have never changed: To love the Lord your God with all your heart, soul, mind, and strength — To love others as yourself — And to live a life that reflects that love in every breath.

Introduction

This book is not a lecture. It's a conversation — an honest, sacred one between hearts that love God and are still learning what that love truly means. It's for those who have studied the Scriptures, served faithfully, and still wonder, *Is this really the heart of God?* It's for those who loved the Church but were wounded by it, and for those who left its walls but not the faith.

This is a book about rediscovering the simplicity of loving God and loving others — even when our theology, traditions, and experiences don't agree. The conversation ahead may stretch your thinking while soothing your heart. Because beneath every disagreement is a truth that will not change: God is love — and love is enough.

We live in a world growing louder and more divided, and even the Church has often reflected that division instead of healing it. We create categories for those who think, worship, vote, or interpret Scripture differently — forgetting we are all still learning to see through the same "glass dimly."

But what if theology wasn't meant to divide us, but to help us see how deeply we need one another? What if the Church could once again be known — not for what it resists — but for what it reflects? This is that invitation: to trade certainty for curiosity, hostility for humility, and argument for Christlikeness.

Read this slowly and prayerfully, as if we were sharing coffee and conversation. Some chapters may affirm what you believe; others may stretch it. That's part of spiritual growth. Pause to pray, reflect, and ask God what He wants to reveal about His love. The goal isn't to finish the book — but to let the book finish something in you.

Ahead, we'll walk through difficult but necessary territory — how theology evolved, how it divided, and how it can become a language of unity again. We'll explore the Church's beauty and brokenness and meet biblical figures not as distant saints, but as humans who wrestled with doubt, ego, and misunderstanding. Through them, we see that God still uses imperfect people to reveal perfect love.

There will be tender moments and convicting ones. But at the center is this truth: Love is the point and the purpose. Love cannot be studied from afar; it must be lived — in forgiveness, in community, in everyday conversations.

So approach each idea with curiosity. Ask God to soften what is hard and illuminate what is true. We are all learners, all students of grace. Whether your path has been inside church walls or outside them, you are seen, known, and loved by the God who delights in being discovered again and again.

This isn't just my story — it's ours. It's the story of a Church awakening to love, of believers learning to disagree with grace, and of souls remembering that faith is not about getting everything right — but about loving like Jesus.

My prayer is simple: that these words transform your heart, giving you courage to love where others divide, hope where others despair, and peace where others argue. If love is the beginning and end of all theology, then every page should lead us back to Him.

Beloved, let us love one another, for love is from God; and everyone who loves is born of God and knows God.
— 1 John 4:7

Chapter 1
The Message Behind the Thought

I've always loved learning. I love studying Scripture—seeing how each part of the Bible connects, exploring the Greek and Hebrew, and digging into the meaning of passages within their context. Learning has always brought me joy. But along the way, I realized that even something as beautiful as theology can become its own form of idolatry.

We can study God so much that we forget to love Him. We can debate His nature while missing His presence. We can memorize His words but lose His tone. I'll never forget the day I prayed, "God, I love You more and understand You less than I ever have." And I meant it. That prayer marked a turning point in my faith—a shift from trying to master the things of God to simply wanting to know Him.

Soon after, I was reminded of Paul's words in 1 Corinthians 13, where he admits that we only "know in part" and see "as in a mirror, dimly." Even Paul—the apostle who shaped much of our understanding—acknowledged he didn't see the full picture. His humility invited me to take the same posture: to hold truth with reverence instead of certainty, and to let mystery make me teachable again.

From that posture came both conviction and peace. Conviction, because I realized how much energy I had spent trying to articulate what I believed instead of simply living it. Peace, because I remembered that faith was never about knowing everything—it was about trusting the One who does.

Theology is beautiful, but incomplete. It gives language to the mystery, but can never replace the mystery itself. And if we want to understand how people who love the same God can disagree so passionately, we have to look backward—not to blame, but to learn.

Almost as soon as the Church was born, believers were already navigating differences. The first followers of Jesus were passionate, imperfect people learning how to walk with Him together. They prayed, broke bread, shared what they had, and carried the story of Jesus wherever they went—but they also wrestled, debated, and questioned.

In Acts, the early apostles faced one of their first major conflicts—a moment when they had to choose whether to make faith harder or simpler for new believers. James reminded them not to make it difficult for those turning to God. Grace was chosen over control. Love was chosen over rules. The path of faith was cleared instead of cluttered.

From the beginning, following Jesus was meant to be about love. Cultures changed, traditions changed, and the Church changed with them. But the heart of Jesus has not changed.

History is not our shame; it's our teacher. When we look back, we learn how to love better. And the same Spirit who moved in Acts 2 is still moving today.

Every branch, denomination, and reform movement grows from the same living root: Jesus Christ. Before theology, before councils, before cathedrals, there was a carpenter who called twelve ordinary people to walk with Him, love one another, and carry His presence into the world.

Jesus used the image of a vine and branches to describe this connection. In John 15, He tells us that He is the vine and we are the branches, and that the only way to bear lasting fruit is to remain connected to Him. Everything that came after—the arguments, the revivals, the reforms—were simply branches trying to describe the same vine. Even when the branches bent in different directions, the root never changed.

When we understand our spiritual lineage, we stop seeing other believers as competitors and start seeing them as kin. The Church is not a collection of rivals but a family tree nourished by the same grace. And if you trace your faith far enough back, you won't find a denomination—you'll find a man named Jesus. The point and the purpose have always been the same: to love God, love others, and stay connected to the root that gives us life.

Paul echoed this in Colossians, urging believers to continue walking in Christ, rooted and built up in Him, strengthened in the faith they had been taught. Our faith doesn't stand because of a label, a tradition, or a branch on the family tree—it stands because we are rooted in Christ Himself. He is the beginning and the continuation of our story, the One who shapes our identity and strengthens our steps.

When we ground our lives in Him, we grow in ways no denomination could ever contain. He becomes our source, stability, and direction. And as we stay rooted in His love, we bear the kind of fruit that reveals where we came from—and who we belong to.

Chapter 2
The Simplicity of Knowing God

Coming out of all my learning about roots, branches, and the heart behind it all, I began noticing something within myself: even with a sincere desire to stay connected to Christ, it was still possible to drift into knowing about God more than actually knowing Him. That realization didn't come in a dramatic moment—it unfolded slowly, the way distance often does.

When I started seminary, I was hungry for truth. I wanted to know everything about God—how He worked, why He allowed what He allowed, what His Word really meant. I wanted to understand the details of His mind and the depths of His ways. And I loved every minute of it. Every lecture felt like a treasure hunt. Every theological discussion felt like standing at the edge of revelation. I filled notebooks with Greek and Hebrew words, historical context, and cultural parallels—all the little puzzle pieces promising to reveal a bigger picture.

I thought the more I learned, the closer I would feel to God. But somewhere along the way, I realized something unsettling: I knew more about Him, but I didn't necessarily know Him more. At first, I didn't notice the distance growing. It happened the way you can live in the same house with someone but slowly stop hearing their voice.

My prayers became essays. My worship became analysis. My Bible reading became preparation for assignments instead of conversations with the Living Word. I was surrounded by people who loved God deeply—and yet, sometimes, it felt like we were dissecting the divine instead of encountering Him. Theology became my map, but at times we forgot to follow the road.

One day in class, listening to another debate about a minor theological point, I prayed quietly, "God, I love You more and understand You less than I ever have." That wasn't frustration—it was humility. Every discussion revealed how much I didn't know; every angle added another layer of mystery. But instead of feeling discouraged, I felt strangely free. My learning had brought me to the edge of something I couldn't master—and wasn't meant to.

Even the Apostle Paul—one of history's greatest theologians—admitted he didn't have it all figured out. He saw only in part. (1 Corinthians 13:12)
The less I could explain, the more I could worship. The less I could define, the more I could trust. It wasn't ignorance—it was intimacy. When I finally

accepted I didn't have to understand everything, my relationship with God began to change. I stopped approaching Him like a professor and started approaching Him like a friend. Theology didn't lose its importance—it simply found its place.

We walk with partial sight because God invites us to trust, not to control. If you've ever tried to follow God and ended up confused, you're in good company. Scripture is filled with people who walked faithfully without seeing clearly. Faith isn't a spotlight revealing the entire path—it's a candle giving just enough light for the next step. And that's how God prefers it. Because if we could see everything, we'd stop needing Him.

There's freedom in admitting we don't know everything—that even our deepest theology is still incomplete. Humility doesn't weaken faith; it protects it. When you know you only see in part, you stop pretending you have it all figured out.

One of the hardest lessons I've learned is that God's faithfulness doesn't depend on my theological accuracy. For years, I believed good theology meant having the right answers—that if I could explain God correctly, I could represent Him perfectly. But here's the truth I've come to cherish: our theology may be flawed, but God's love never is.

The problem isn't theology; it's pride. When being right becomes more important than being kind, we stop reflecting the God we claim to defend. And pride isn't something a classroom can correct—only the Spirit can.

Looking back on my journey, I can see how my theology has changed many times, yet God's commitment never wavered. He isn't offended by our process; He meets us in it. The more I've studied Church history, the more I've seen this pattern in others too. People with sincere hearts and imperfect theology still changed the world—Luther, Wesley, Mother Teresa—each reflecting a piece of God's perfection through human imperfection. We are all cracked vessels, but light often shines best through cracks.

The goal of theology was never to win debates—it was always to reveal the character of the One who cannot be contained by them. We will never have perfect theology, but we can have perfect love. Because one day, when we finally see Him face to face, our theology will fall silent—and love will still be speaking.

Chapter 3
The Theology of Love

As my understanding of God shifted from knowledge to relationship, another truth began to unfold — one that touched not just how I knew God, but how I represented Him. All the learning in the world, all the humility gained along the way, meant very little if love wasn't shaping the way I spoke, taught, and lived. That realization began to change the way I saw ministry altogether.

There was a season when I believed my role was to point out what was wrong — wrong beliefs, wrong behaviors, wrong choices. I preached with passion and conviction, convinced I was defending truth, but I didn't realize how much joy it was quietly draining from my soul. The more I preached about what I was against, the less room I had to celebrate what I was for. Sermons became battle plans. Altar calls felt like interventions. Without meaning to, I began seeing people through the lens of correction instead of compassion.

The heaviness that comes from fighting battles God never asked you to fight is exhausting. And it was in that exhaustion that I finally heard the still, small voice of God: "Cindy, I never called you to preach what you stand against. From now on, preach what you stand for."

For months, I wasn't sure how to preach at all. I had spent years using Scripture like a sword, helping people come to God through fear, guilt, and a long list of what they had done wrong. Suddenly, all I had were a few Scriptures and a trembling heart. The words didn't flow the way they used to, but the tears did. I was learning a new language — the language of love. And love doesn't shout. It invites.

Preaching what you're against comes naturally to the flesh; it gives the illusion of control. But preaching what you're for requires surrender. It means trusting that truth, spoken in love, can accomplish what condemnation never could.

When I began preaching what I stood for — grace, mercy, reconciliation, kindness, justice, hope — something shifted in the room. I realized people don't change because they're told what's wrong with them. They change when they're reminded how valuable they are to God. They change because they encounter the One who gives life.

That whisper — "Preach what you stand for" — is still the compass of my calling. It reminds me that theology was never meant to be a weapon; it was always meant to be a window into the heart of God. Sermons are not battles to win but bridges to build. And the most powerful message I will ever preach isn't a statement — it's a life lived in love.

I've learned the difference between a wound and a scar is time, and the difference between a message that hurts and a message that heals is love. For years, I didn't realize my words, though intended to help, sometimes left wounds. As I learned to preach what I stood for, my messages shifted. Instead of saying, "You're broken," I began saying, "You're loved." Instead of "You've failed," I began saying, "You're forgiven." Instead of "You're far from God," I began saying, "He's never left your side."

When your life radiates grace, people hear your words differently. When you lead with compassion, people begin to believe again — not just in God, but in themselves.

Love isn't an accessory to the gospel — it is the gospel. And since that shift, I've watched God heal more through gentleness than I ever saw through judgment. Healing is never loud. It's steady, it's faithful, and it doesn't come through the thunder of correction but through the whisper of compassion.

John wrote that God is love, and Paul reminded us that love never fails. These truths are the foundation of every theology worth keeping. Trace any theological thread far enough, and you will find love is the point and love is the purpose.

Love will always offend systems that prefer control. It is too simple for scholars, too generous for the self-righteous, too wild for those who cling to order. But love was never meant to fit inside doctrine; doctrine was meant to point us toward love.

Love makes theology human. It takes divine truth and wraps it in skin so people can recognize it. It takes abstract grace and turns it into practical compassion. And when the theology of love touches real lives, the world begins to heal.

When I meet God face to face, I'm not expecting a theological exam. I believe He will ask one question: "Did you love well?" And I want my life — not just my sermons and not just my theology — to answer yes.

Because everything I've learned, everything I've unlearned, everything I've taught, and everything I've lived has led me here: Love. It is the beginning, the middle, and the end. And when all our voices fade and the world grows quiet, love will still be speaking.

As love became the lens through which I understood God, it also became the lens through which I began to understand people. It made me see not only what love asks of me, but why God designed us the way He did. And that realization led me into the next part of this journey — a question that had been quietly waiting beneath the surface: If love is the heartbeat of God's design, why did He make us all so different?

Chapter 4
Made Different on Purpose

Love had begun to reshape my theology, my preaching, and the way I moved through the world. But as that shift settled deeper into my heart, it awakened a question I had never fully explored. If the gospel is the good news of God's love poured out through Jesus — a love meant to heal, restore, and unite — then why did God create humanity with such stunning variety?

Why give us personalities, strengths, perspectives, and temperaments that don't always fit neatly together? Why not make relationship easier?

The truth is, God never intended sameness.
His design was diversity wrapped in love.

Humanity was born from the relational heart of God. When God said, "Let Us make humankind in Our image," He wasn't just speaking of function — He was speaking of reflection. Father, Son, and Spirit — perfect unity, perfect love — created people not out of need but out of overflowing affection. And He stamped that divine image into every human being.

But the image of God is far too vast, too vibrant, too multifaceted to be captured in one kind of person. God didn't craft us from a single mold. He didn't duplicate us. Instead, He wove different threads of His nature into each one of us — creativity, compassion, wit, insight, tenderness, strength, resilience. No one person reflects the fullness of God, but each of us reflects something true about Him.

We were not accidentally formed.
We were not randomly assembled.
We were not standardized.

We were fearfully made.
Wonderfully made.
Intentionally, individually made.

Our uniqueness is not a defect.
It is a declaration of divine craftsmanship.

And difference was never the problem.

When love is in place, difference becomes a gift.
It enriches.
It strengthens.
It reveals more of God.
It invites us into relationships where we need one another, not to survive, but to see more clearly.

This was God's desire from the beginning: a world of diverse people, living in harmony, each bearing a facet of His image.

But when humanity drifted away from God's love, our differences — meant to draw us together — began to tear us apart. Without love grounding us, uniqueness became a reason for comparison, fear, conflict, and control.

Differences in culture became division.
Differences in power became oppression.
Differences in belief became war.
Differences in perspective became broken relationships.

Not because difference is wrong —
but because love was lost.

Even the early believers struggled with this. Paul had to remind them that they were one body with many members, each part necessary, each part intentionally placed. They weren't being introduced to a new teaching — they were being called back to the original design. Through Christ, God was restoring what had been fractured.

Because difference without love divides.
Difference with love displays the beauty of the One who made us.

And then Jesus came and showed us what this looks like in real life.

He didn't gather a group of identical people. He called fiery Peter and gentle John, educated Matthew and skeptical Thomas, young zealots and older fishermen — men who never would have chosen one another. Jesus didn't erase their differences. He taught them how to love within them.

He was tender with the broken.
Patient with the unsure.
Strong with the proud.
Direct with those who used religion to burden others.

Jesus revealed what humanity grounded in love was always meant to look like — beautifully diverse, uniquely gifted, fearfully made, yet held together by compassion.

This chapter sits between where we've been and where we're going for a reason. Before we can explore how love reshapes our communities and our relationships, we must first understand why love is necessary in the first place.

God's love gives meaning to our differences.
God's love gives purpose to our uniqueness.
God's love makes harmony possible.

Without love, difference divides.
With love, difference becomes divine.

God made us different on purpose.
He made us unique with intention.
He made us in His image — with love as the binding force that brings it all together.

And when we stand on that love, everything God intended — unity, connection, purpose — becomes possible again.

This is the natural doorway to what comes next. Because if God designed us to reflect His image uniquely, then the way we come together in love is how the world sees that image most clearly. Love doesn't just shape individuals — it shapes communities. And that is where the journey leads now.

That invitation became the beginning of our spiritual family tree—a story rooted in love, shaped by grace, and carried across generations. And to understand the beauty of the Church today, we have to trace those roots.

Chapter 5
Love Recognized

If the theology of love forms the foundation of our faith, then the way we love one another is where that theology begins to take shape in the world. Jesus said the world would recognize His disciples by one thing—the way we love. Not by sermons or systems or styles of worship, but by love. If love shapes our hearts, then community becomes the place where that love becomes visible.

Love was never meant to stay private. Jesus didn't draw people into isolated spiritual paths; He formed a community. He called individuals, yes, but He immediately brought them into relationships where love could be practiced, shared, stretched, and proven. He knew that love becomes its strongest witness not in solitude, but in togetherness.

A theology of love becomes a community of love. And a community of love becomes a testimony the world cannot ignore.

Jesus often reminded His followers that where two or three gather in His name, He is present among them. His presence doesn't require crowds or platforms; it rests wherever love gathers. It rests wherever people choose to walk with one another in kindness, humility, and grace.

Love draws us to Jesus personally. Community shapes us collectively. And when community is formed by love, that love begins to move outward.

The earliest believers understood this. Their gatherings were simple: shared meals, prayers, conversations, and friendship. Nothing flashy. Nothing complicated. They didn't meet to consume; they met to connect. They didn't show up to be spectators; they showed up to belong. And their love for one another became a quiet but powerful testimony that drew people toward God.

Community is where what we believe becomes how we live. It's where forgiveness stops being theory and becomes practice. It's where grace becomes a culture, not a concept.

Today the forms of church vary—large gatherings, small groups, living rooms, coffee shops—but the heart of community remains unchanged. Jesus never said His presence would be strongest in cathedrals or conferences. He said He would be with us when a few gather in His name. That means church can happen anywhere love takes root.

Wherever love gathers, the Church becomes visible.
Community doesn't have to be organized to be holy.
It doesn't have to be polished to be powerful.
It just has to be real.

As the world shifts, the Church is rediscovering this simplicity. We are learning again that the strength of our faith isn't measured by attendance or programs, but by presence. By belonging. By love. This is not the loss of the Church—it is the return of the Church to its beginning.

Community doesn't just strengthen us; it prepares us to carry love into the world. Because the theology of love was never meant to stay within our gatherings. It was meant to move outward—to workplaces, families, neighborhoods, and conversations where love has grown thin.

When believers walk in love together, people encounter something unexpected: hope instead of judgment, compassion instead of distance, gentleness instead of condemnation. A community formed by love becomes a doorway for the hurting to experience God.

The world does not need a Church that shouts louder. It needs a Church that loves deeper.

A Church that listens, that heals, that forgives, that welcomes. A Church that reflects the heart of Jesus not just in doctrine, but in daily life.

Some communities begin with a handful of people praying. Others begin around tables or through simple messages of encouragement. The size never determines the strength—love does. Jesus didn't say, "Where the crowd is big, I am with them." He said, "Where two or three gather, I am there."

When we choose to walk together with authenticity and grace, we become a living testimony. We reflect the kingdom in ordinary ways that speak louder than any sermon. We show the world what Jesus looks like—not by perfection, but by presence.

And as this kind of community grows, something else happens: our hearts start to widen. Love practiced in community becomes love carried into the world. We begin noticing needs we once overlooked. We feel compassion we once ignored. We start becoming the kind of people who bring love wherever we go.

This is the Church Jesus envisioned—built not on control, but on compassion; not on hierarchy, but on humility; not on isolation, but on belonging. Love turns walls into windows and strangers into family.

A theology of love becomes a community of love. A community of love becomes a movement of love. And a movement of love becomes a healing force in a divided world.

Every community has a story. Every gathering of believers comes from a long line of people who said yes to Jesus, even imperfectly. Before we can talk about how to live the gospel today, it helps to understand where our story began and what our spiritual family has walked through.

Because the way we see God—and the way we see each other—has roots far deeper than we often realize.

Chapter 6

When Love Was the Beginning: The Story We All Inherited

If we're going to understand how to live the gospel today, we have to take a moment to look at where we came from.

Every one of us carries a spiritual story we didn't choose—one handed down through generations of believers who loved God, struggled, misunderstood, hoped, feared, and kept walking anyway. We inherit more than doctrine; we inherit patterns, instincts, assumptions, and ways of seeing the world. And when we understand where those things come from, something beautiful happens: we begin to see ourselves with compassion instead of confusion.

We begin to see our spiritual family not as a fractured history but as a long journey of people trying to return to the love they were made for.

Because whether we realize it or not, our story didn't begin with division.

It began with love.

Love at the Beginning

Before there were church buildings or sermons or systems, before anyone argued about theology or leadership, there was a God whose very nature is love. Out of that love, humanity was created—crafted in His image, designed for relationship, made to live in unity with Him and with one another.

Love was our first environment. It was the air we breathed. It was the language our souls understood.

We knew who we were because we knew who God was. Our identity was rooted in love. That was our beginning.

When the Human Condition Emerged

But somewhere along the way, something shifted. Humanity stepped out of the love that shaped us, and the human condition emerged: fear, shame, pride, comparison, insecurity, and the instinct to control what we cannot understand.

The moment love was replaced with fear, everything changed. We began to see one another through suspicion instead of trust. We began to protect ourselves instead of offering ourselves. We began to gather around similarities instead of embracing differences. This wasn't because God withdrew His love—it was because we stopped trusting it.

And every time humanity forgets love, we see the same patterns repeat: misunderstanding, division, hierarchy, rivalry, and the need to prove ourselves or protect ourselves. These dynamics didn't begin in the modern world. They began in the human heart, long before the Church ever existed.

A Family Story of Forgetting & Remembering Love

When Jesus entered history, He stepped into a world full of religious devotion yet weighed down by spiritual pressure. People loved God deeply, but they had inherited systems that sometimes obscured His true heart. Traditions meant to lead them toward love had slowly become burdens too heavy to carry.

Jesus didn't reject their heritage—He restored it. He brought them back to the love they were made for. He showed them what God had always been like. He revealed who they had always been. He held up a mirror that reflected love instead of shame.

And when He gathered His disciples, He didn't choose people who naturally fit together. He chose men from different backgrounds, temperaments, and perspectives. They did not always understand one another. They did not always agree. They wrestled with jealousy, insecurity, competition, and fear. They were spiritual family long before they were spiritually mature. Just like us, they had to learn how to love each other along the way.

Church History Through the Lens of Love

After Jesus returned to the Father, the early Church carried His message forward—but they also carried their humanity with them. They struggled. They argued. They misunderstood each other. They brought their cultural, personal, and spiritual baggage into the community God was forming.

Yet through it all, love kept calling them forward. Over time, different expressions of faith emerged:

Some believers gravitated toward tradition and reverence.
Some toward Scripture and clarity.
Some toward mystery and worship.
Some toward freedom and simplicity.
Some toward structure and order.

Some toward renewal and the movement of the Spirit.
Some toward service and justice.

Each stream held part of the picture—but none held the whole.

And woven through all of it was the same pattern: When the Church drifted away from love, God gently invited them back.

Every renewal movement, every reformation, every revival was ultimately a return to love—a rediscovery of grace, compassion, humility, and the heart of God.

This means church history is not primarily a story of conflict—it is a story of God refusing to let His people forget love.

Your Spiritual Ancestry Matters

Whether you grew up Catholic or Protestant, charismatic or contemplative, traditional or modern, you inherited a story that shaped the way you see God, yourself, and the world.

You inherited strengths.
You inherited wounds.
You inherited instincts.

You inherited hesitations.
You inherited hopes.

Some traditions passed down a deep sense of reverence.
Some passed down a passion for Scripture.
Some passed down the power of the Spirit.
Some passed down the discipline of prayer.
Some passed down the gift of service.
Some passed down a culture of shame.
Some passed down fear.
Some passed down striving.
Some passed down performance.
Some passed down joy.

Your spiritual reactions—your longing, your resistance, your hunger, your fears—are not random. They are roots. They have a story. And when you understand that story, you no longer blame yourself for what you inherited—you simply begin to grow beyond it.

Understanding our spiritual ancestry isn't about dividing us. It's about freeing us.

Because once you know where your spiritual patterns came from, you can choose what you keep, what you release, and what you allow God to heal.

Love Never Stops Calling Us Forward

Across every generation, across every expression of the Church, love has been the force that refuses to let the story end in brokenness. It has always been love that restores, love that reconciles, love that revives, love that rebuilds.

Love was the beginning.
Love is the thread.
Love is the invitation.
Love is the destiny.

And now it's our turn.

As we learn to live the gospel today, we don't do it as isolated individuals. We do it as people shaped by a long, complex, beautiful, imperfect spiritual family—a family God has never given up on.

Your story is part of that family.
Your life is another chapter in love's unfolding story.

And now that we understand where we came from, we can begin to understand where God is leading us next.

Chapter 7

Living What You Believe

There comes a moment in every believer's life when faith must take on feet — when the words we've heard, memorized, or inherited must step off the page and begin to walk in the world. You can know Scripture, study theology, and recite all the right answers, but the truest expression of faith is never found in debate. It is found in how you live.

Faith that remains only intellectual eventually becomes theoretical. Faith that is lived becomes transformational. And when we begin to live our faith, something sacred happens: we discover that what we inherited does not have to define what we become.

Every believer carries spiritual instincts shaped by family, tradition, culture, and history. Some of us inherited caution. Some inherited passion. Some inherited discipline. Some inherited shame. These instincts show up in how we respond to God and to others — the instinct to perform, the instinct to withdraw, the instinct to fix, to avoid, to argue, to please, to hide. None of these reflexes are random.

They are part of the story we carry. But inheritance is not destiny.

Living faith means allowing God's love to reshape the reflexes we were handed. It means trading certainty for intimacy — learning to trust even when we don't have all the answers. It means letting who God is become who we are becoming. Theology teaches us who God is. Obedience teaches us what He's like. And over time, our questions shift. We stop asking, "Am I right?" and start asking, "Am I loving well?" Because mature faith doesn't need to prove God. Mature faith begins to reflect Him.

Real faith is not measured by how much we know but by how deeply we love. Micah once summarized the entire posture of a God-shaped life in three simple movements: act justly, love mercy, walk humbly. Justice means doing what is right, not what is convenient. Mercy means compassion even when it costs us. Humility means staying teachable and interruptible before God. These three practices become the rhythm of a faith that is truly alive. And they grow not in dramatic moments, but in ordinary soil.

Most of our spiritual formation happens in unseen moments — choosing kindness over reaction, listening instead of defending, slowing down long enough to notice someone's pain, responding with gentleness when frustration rises. Walking out your faith doesn't mean living perfectly; it means living presently. It means being aware of God in the everyday spaces where life unfolds: at work, in the car, while folding laundry, during hard conversations, when someone misunderstands you. When you live that way, life itself becomes worship.

To walk with God is to walk humbly. Humility is not weakness; it is awareness — the understanding that everything we are and everything we have comes from Him. Pride says, "I know enough." Humility says, "Teach me again." Pride wants to win the argument. Humility wants to win the heart. When humility leads you, you stop seeing people as opponents and start seeing them as image-bearers. You stop needing to be right and start longing to be righteous — not self-righteous, but Spirit-shaped.

Humility makes room for love to lead.

It's easy to say, "I believe in love," until loving costs you something. It's easy to say, "I believe in forgiveness," until forgiveness becomes painful. But this is where faith becomes visible. Walking out your faith means choosing obedience when it's inconvenient, choosing grace when it's undeserved, choosing peace when it would be easier to fight. Every small act of obedience ripples outward. Every quiet yes becomes a sermon without words.

And sometimes walking out your faith looks less like striding and more like crawling — when prayers go unanswered, when doors close, when God feels silent. These aren't signs of weak faith. They are places where faith is being formed. Faith isn't proven when we understand everything. Faith is proven when we trust anyway.

The most powerful ministry you will ever have begins under your own roof. Faith in action means showing the same patience to your family that you offer to strangers. It means offering grace to your spouse when the words come out wrong. It means teaching children that prayer isn't a performance — it's a conversation with the God who loves them. Home is the training ground of the Gospel. It's where humility is practiced, where forgiveness is tested, where love is proven. You don't need a pulpit to preach. You need a table, a listening ear, and a heart that whispers, "As for me and my house, we will serve the Lord."

For most of us, the majority of life happens at work — not in church. And that is not a distraction from your calling; it is part of it. Your workplace is the mission field disguised as routine. When you choose integrity in the face of temptation, you are preaching the Gospel. When you lead with kindness instead of control, you are revealing the heart of Jesus. When you handle conflict with grace instead of gossip, you plant seeds of peace. You carry the Gospel not by quoting Scripture but by embodying it.

Jesus spent His life with the overlooked and the hurting — the ones society avoided, dismissed, or judged. Following Him means going where comfort ends and compassion begins. Faith in action means noticing the unseen, sitting with the lonely, and reminding the forgotten that they are known. Some of the most powerful moments of ministry happen in silence: a whispered prayer in a hospital room, a meal left on a doorstep, a message sent at the right moment, a note tucked into someone's hand. These moments are sermons heaven sees.

There comes a point in every believer's life when the Gospel is no longer just what we speak — it is who we become. People rarely come to Jesus because someone out-argued them. They come because someone loved them. You are a living letter — written not with ink but with the Spirit of God. Your scars hold stories of redemption. Your transformation whispers of His power. Your kindness reveals His heart. Your joy testifies that He is near. Your peace says, "This is what God can do."

When Christ lives through you, He becomes the explanation for everything that doesn't make sense about your life — why you forgive, why you stay gentle, why you choose mercy, why you show up with compassion, why you love people who cannot love you back. This is the Gospel in motion. This is faith that breathes. This is love that lives.

You don't have to transform the world. You simply have to carry the One who already has. So let your life speak. Let your love preach. Let your faith breathe. Because when you become the message, the world begins to see the Messenger.

Chapter 8
Love That Leads

Every believer carries influence, whether they recognize it or not. Leadership is not reserved for titles, platforms, or positions. It is the quiet weight of your presence, the impact of your words, the spirit you carry into a room. Leadership begins the moment your life begins to affect another life — which means every follower of Jesus is a leader in some way.

But in a world obsessed with visibility, authority, and platform, Jesus offers us a different picture. He leads from love, not from power. He shapes hearts by serving, not by controlling. He doesn't climb above others — He stoops low enough to lift them. And in doing so, He shows us what leadership was always meant to be. True leadership is not found in influence gained but in love given.

As we grow in faith, something begins to shift inside us. We realize that leadership isn't about being impressive — it's about being willing. It's about letting God form our hearts until our lives become places where others can encounter His compassion, His wisdom, His patience, His presence. Leadership is love in motion. But before we can lead well, we often have to unlearn what leadership meant to us before love became the center.

Some of us inherited harsh leadership. Some inherited controlling leadership. Some inherited fearful leadership. Some inherited passive leadership. Some inherited leadership that valued results more than people. Some inherited leadership that cared more about image than integrity. And without realizing it, those models become the scripts we follow. But you were never meant to lead out of fear, pride, pressure, or insecurity.

You were meant to lead out of love. Love is the great reorienter. It changes the posture of our hearts before it ever changes the scope of our influence.

Good leadership begins at home — long before it is ever recognized in public. It takes shape in the tone of your voice when the day has exhausted you, in the patience you choose with a child who is struggling, in the forgiveness you extend when someone in your family hurts you. Home is where leadership is tested, refined, stretched, and proven.

The same is true in our friendships. Leadership is found in the friend who listens without judgment, the one who stands beside you in seasons of confusion, the one who calls out the good in you when you've forgotten it yourself. Leadership often begins with the simplest gift: presence.

But for many believers, the greatest portion of leadership plays out in the workplace. That's where integrity matters, where kindness stands out, where patience becomes a witness. The office, the classroom, the job site — these are not places separate from your calling. They are woven into it. When you choose honesty when no one would have known otherwise, you are preaching the Gospel.

When you respond with gentleness in a tense room, you are leading with Christ's heart. When you refuse gossip and choose grace, you plant seeds of peace. You carry the Gospel not by quoting Scripture, but by embodying it. Leadership is not a stage. It is a way of being. And the leaders who most reflect Christ are not the ones who shout the loudest but the ones who love the deepest.

Jesus led in ways that confounded the world around Him. He touched the untouchable. He dignified the overlooked. He restored those religion had cast aside. He corrected without shaming, guided without controlling, and spoke truth without losing tenderness. Every miracle He performed, every conversation He held, every step He took revealed a God whose authority flowed from love. This is the model we follow. Leadership shaped by love looks like humility — the willingness to listen, to learn, to apologize, to grow. It looks like courage — the boldness to speak truth when silence would be safer.

It looks like compassion — the ability to see someone's pain even when they hide it. It looks like integrity — alignment between what we believe and how we behave. And it looks like surrender — trusting God to lead us so that we can lead others well.

There will be moments when leadership feels heavy — when the people you serve misunderstand you, when the path forward is unclear, when the cost of doing what is right feels higher than you expected. These moments do not disqualify you. They develop you.

Leadership is shaped not by ease but by obedience. Sometimes leading with love means standing firm when others want you to bend. Sometimes it means stepping back when your ego wants you to step forward. Sometimes it means being the first to forgive, the first to listen, the first to soften. None of these come naturally; all of them come through surrender. And the leadership God forms in you will not always be visible.

Some of the most powerful leadership happens where no one sees: in quiet prayers whispered over your children, in unseen sacrifices you make for your family, in silent battles you fight to choose kindness, faithfulness, gentleness, or restraint. Heaven sees these moments. Heaven celebrates them. Because love that leads in secret becomes strength that leads in public.

You don't have to be perfect to lead. You only have to be willing to let God shape your heart. The Spirit who dwells within you empowers you to lead in ways you never could on your own. He softens what is harsh, strengthens what is weak, steadies what is fearful, and purifies what is selfish. He forms Christ within you so Christ can be seen through you.

This is what leadership in the kingdom looks like: God working through ordinary people in ordinary moments, transforming ordinary spaces with extraordinary love.

Your influence is not measured by how many people follow you but by how many people encounter God because of you. Leadership is not about rising above others. Leadership is about rising to love others.

When love becomes the way you lead — in your home, in your friendships, in your workplace, in your church, in your conversations, in your unseen moments — the world begins to catch a glimpse of the Leader who lives within you. And that is the kind of leadership that leaves a legacy. Not a legacy of achievement, but a legacy of love.

Chapter 9

Living the Message Beyond the Pages

There comes a moment in every believer's journey when the truths we've learned begin to move beyond understanding and start shaping the way we live. Faith stops being something we simply admire and becomes something we embody. The Gospel was never meant to stay on the page. It was always meant to take on flesh again through people who have been transformed by love — people like you. It is easy to talk about love, sing about love, and study love.

But the true power of the Gospel is revealed when love becomes the way we respond in ordinary moments, the way we speak to those who misunderstand us, the way we forgive, the way we slow down enough to see others, the way we choose gentleness when we feel justified in being harsh. Love is not proven in statements. It is proven in steps. It becomes visible through our patience, our presence, our compassion, and the quiet integrity of our daily choices.

You carry a message within you — one written not with ink but with the Spirit of God. He has written it through your healing, your surrender, your growth, your resilience, your repentance, and your hope. Your life tells a story of a God who did not give up on you, who carried you when you were weary, who corrected you gently, who waited patiently, who loved you through every stage of becoming. The world is not changed by people who know love exists, but by people who allow love to shape who they are. The world doesn't need more arguments for God; it needs more evidence of Him. And that evidence comes through lives transformed.

Every time you choose mercy instead of retaliation, you preach the Gospel. Every time you choose humility instead of pride, you reveal the heart of Jesus. Every time you choose to listen rather than defend, or to forgive rather than hold onto a wound, the Gospel becomes visible through you. Your life is the sermon some people will never hear from a pulpit but will read in the way you treat them. People may debate theology, but they cannot deny kindness. They cannot dismiss compassion. They cannot ignore the quiet strength of someone who carries peace into difficult places.

You don't have to travel far to live this message. You don't need a stage or a spotlight. Your home is a sanctuary. Your workplace is a mission field. Your friendships are sacred ground. Your daily routines are opportunities for grace. The places where you feel unseen may be the very places where God does His greatest work in you and through you. Living the message means living aware — aware that every conversation holds an opportunity, every interruption may be an invitation, every burden someone carries is a chance to reveal the gentleness of Christ.

The beauty of the Gospel is that it does not demand perfection; it invites surrender. God is not asking you to impress Him. He is asking you to trust Him. To let Him shape your heart so deeply that love becomes your reflex. The Spirit who lives within you empowers you to live in ways you never could on your own. He strengthens what is weak in you, softens what has hardened, steadies what is fearful, and purifies what is selfish. He forms Christ in you so Christ can be seen through you.

You may never know how many lives your faithfulness touches. You may never see the seeds you plant become fruit. But every word of encouragement, every act of compassion, every moment of selfless love becomes part of a story God is writing — a story far larger than your own. Sometimes the most powerful Gospel moments are the ones no one sees: a whispered prayer, a quiet act of service, a gentle response that defuses tension, a choice to stay kind when the world expects you to break.

Living the message means becoming a living reminder of the love that changed you. When your joy does not depend on circumstances, when your peace cannot be shaken by storms, when your mercy surprises those who expected anger, people encounter God. Not because you are extraordinary, but because He is present in you. This is the miracle of the Gospel — Christ in you, the hope of glory.

As you move forward from these pages, remember that the message does not end here. It continues through your life, your presence, your love. Wherever you go — into healing, into work, into ministry, into relationships, into uncertainty — you carry the heart of Jesus with you. And as long as love leads you, you will never walk without purpose.

Let your life speak. Let your love preach. Let your faith breathe. Because when you become the message, the world begins to recognize the Messenger. And each morning, let your heart begin with a simple prayer: "God, what are You doing today — and how can I help?"

Epilogue

The Endless Story of Love

There are no real endings when it comes to love. Only new beginnings, quiet continuations, and the steady echo of grace that keeps moving long after the last page is turned. If this book has been anything, I pray it has reminded you not of what separates us, but of what holds us together. Not of what has fractured our story, but of what God still longs to restore. Not of all we struggle to understand, but of the One who understands us completely and still chooses us with joy.

Love is the language of heaven. It is the thread woven through creation, through Scripture, through history, and through your own life. It is the river that has been quietly shaping you long before you had words for it. And at some point in every journey of faith, we arrive at a moment like this — where you close a book, not because the message is over, but because it is beginning to form in you in a new way.

What you've read here was never meant to stay contained within chapters. It was meant to move — through your voice, your presence, your decisions, your relationships, your community. You are a continuation of this message. Your compassion, your courage, your faithfulness, and your willingness to love in difficult places will speak to hearts that sermons will never reach.

Paul once wrote that we "see in part," and that truth will follow us all our days. We will never hold every answer. Our theology will always contain mystery. Our interpretations will sometimes disagree. But love — love remains when understanding fails. Love bridges the gaps our minds cannot. Love carries us when certainty collapses. Love reminds us that God did not call us to win arguments; He called us to win hearts.

One day, in the fullness of eternity, everything we hold in fragments will be made whole. Every misunderstanding will dissolve. Every wound will be healed. Every division will be mended by the brilliance of perfect love. Until that day comes, love is our truest compass. It points us toward God, toward one another, and toward the person we are becoming.

If you carry one truth from these pages, let it be this: You are deeply loved by God, and you were created to love deeply in return. Wherever you go next — into work, into ministry, into healing, into questions, into new seasons of becoming — take love with you. Take it into conversations. Take it into conflict. Take it into grief and into joy. Let it soften what the world has hardened. Let it hold you when certainty slips through your fingers. Let it define you when labels fall away.

May your faith grow gentler. May your theology bow to compassion. May your ministry overflow with mercy. May your heart stay tender in a world that rewards hardness. And may your life reveal what words alone never could — that love was always the point, and love will always lead us home.

Amen. And amen again.

About the Author

Cindy H. Carr began her faith journey on December 24, 1984. It didn't begin in a church service or with an altar call, but through a personal invitation from Jesus Christ while she was alone preparing for Christmas Eve. In that quiet moment, a relationship was born—one that transcended theology, tradition, and every expectation of what faith was "supposed" to be.

Over the decades that followed, Cindy immersed herself in theological study and served in both business and her community, yet her unwavering relationship with Jesus Christ has guided every step of her life and leadership. She has learned that love—steady, simple, and sincere—is the foundation strong enough to endure any storm.

In *What's the Point, What's the Purpose*, Cindy steps beyond titles, roles, and traditions to share a message rooted in the same love that transformed her life. In a world where faith and culture often feel complicated and divided, she calls readers back to what is essential: the love of God that brings clarity, connection, and peace. With a compassionate, grounded voice, she invites us to quiet the noise, return to the heart of faith, and see life—and one another—through the lens of unwavering love.

Visit Cindy's website to view her full catalog of books, or scan the QR code to access them all on Amazon.

www.cindyhcarr.com

ANCHORS
for
ADHD

A Stability Guide for
People Living with ADHD

Cindy H. Carr, D.Min., MACL
The Anchored Series

ANCHORS
for
ANXIETY

A Stability Guide for
People Living With Anxiety

Cindy H. Carr, D.Min., MACL
The Anchored Series

ANCHORS
for
BIPOLAR DISORDER

A Stability Guide for
People Living With Bipolar Disorder

Cindy H. Carr, D.Min., MACL
The Anchored Series

ANCHORS
for
PANIC DISORDER

A Stability Guide for
People Living With Panic Disorder

Cindy H. Carr, D.Min., MACL
The Anchored Series

ANCHORS
for
PTSD

A Stability Guide for
People Living with Post-Traumatic Stress Disorder

Cindy H. Carr, D.Min., MACL
The Anchored Series

ANCHORS
for
MAJOR DEPRESSIVE DISORDER

A Stability Guide for
People Living With Major Depressive Disorder

Cindy H. Carr, D.Min., MACL
The Anchored Series

ANCHORS
of
FAITH

Walking with God Through Mental Illness, One Ordinary Day at a Time

Cindy H. Carr, D.Min., MACL
The Anchored Series

ANCHORS
of
SUPPORT

Building a Legacy of Stability for Families Navigating Mental Illness

Cindy H. Carr, D.Min., MACL
The Anchored Series

Support
WITHOUT
Drowning
When Addiction Shows Up

Cindy H. Carr, D.Min., MACL

OUR
HOME
Us

Building A Legacy of Love

Cindy H. Carr, D.Min., MACL

www.ingramcontent.com/pod-product-compliance
Lightning Source LLC
LaVergne TN
LVHW010841120826
845149LV00020B/3452
* 9 7 8 1 9 7 1 1 9 2 0 0 0 *